Friendly Street

NEW POETS 17

Friendly Street
NEW POETS 17

Fence Music • John Pfitzner

Gunyah *Healing* • gareth roi jones

Sliding Down the Belly of the World • Rachael Mead

§

Friendly Street Poets

Friendly Street Poets Inc.
PO Box 3697
Norwood SA 5067
friendlystreetpoets.org.au

Wakefield Press
1 The Parade West
Kent Town
South Australia 5067
www.wakefieldpress.com.au

First published 2012

Cover photograph by Chris Ide – Cideway Imagery www.cideway.com.au
Cover design by Clinton Ellicott, Wakefield Press, and
Thom Sullivan, Friendly Street Poets Inc.
Typeset by Clinton Ellicott, Wakefield Press
Edited by Thom Sullivan, Friendly Street Poets Inc.
Printed in Australia by Griffin Digital, Adelaide

ISBN 978 1 74305 101 6

Government
of South Australia

Arts SA

Friendly Street Poets Inc. is supported
by the **South Australian Government**
through **Arts SA.**

fox creek
wines

Contents

Edited by
Thom Sullivan

Fence Music

John Pfitzner

John Pfitzner studied English and Classical Greek at the University of Adelaide and theology at Immanuel Seminary, North Adelaide. By profession he has been a minister of religion and a publishing house editor.

He played Australian Rules football for West Adelaide in the SANFL and has completed four marathons.

For fifteen years he, his wife Diana and their three children lived at Hermannsburg NT, where he learnt the local Aboriginal language.

His interests, besides poetry, include reading, films, music, sketching, birdwatching, human rights and spirituality.

Acknowledgements

'The Wrong Grave' received a commendation in the Max Harris Poetry Award 2008. 'Judith' appeared in *After the Race: Friendly Street Poets 34*; 'Galileo's Telescope' in *Sorcerers and Soothsayers: Friendly Street Poets 35*; 'Fence Music' in *Dodecahedron: Poets Union Anthology 2010*; 'Man on Wire' in *Season of a New Heart: Poets Corner Anthology*; 'Deus Absconditus' in *Studio* (Number 118); 'Stealth' in *InDaily* (30 September 2011). 'To Soar' was Friendly Street Poets Poem of the Month, October 2011.

Thank You
To Poets Corner at the Effective Living Centre and its convenors Sean Gilbert and Mary Taylor; Poetica and its convenor Krishan Persaud; Friendly Street Poets and its convenor Maggie Emmett.

Dedication
To Jude Aquilina, for getting me started on the journey and David Adès, for accompanying me on the way.

Contents

Judith

We came to expect it of her
but it still astonished us –
her noticing of need
and her quickness to see
what she could do to meet it.
What we saw in her
was an instinct for empathy,
a compassion reflex,
fluency in the language of acceptance,
a grasp of the grammar
of the spontaneous act of kindness.

In Varanasi, rugged up
against the pre-dawn chill,
we stepped ashore
after a boat ride on the Ganges
viewing the ghats.
When she saw the oarsman rub his hands,
it seemed to her his need
was greater than hers
and on impulse she turned back
and gave him her gloves.
And because she was tall
and he was slim,
and because she was human
and had seen that he was too,
the gloves fitted.

Somewhere I've Never Been Before

I am going to select a six-speed Softail Harley
all sleek slinky low-slung silver and black.
I am going to sit loose in the saddle, hands wide
on the handlebars, feet firm on the footboards.
I want to feel that choppy potato-potato sound
growling up through my leather-clad body.
I want to greet other Harley riders with
a subtle lift of a finger, be part of the club.
I want to own the road, glide the highway
breathe sun-laden rain-scented air
slide the kilometres under my wheels
find myself somewhere I've never been before.

Galileo's Telescope

It could be just a toy
or the latest advance in military technology,
but when he aims it at the heavens
the whole cosmos is shaken.
Earth begins to spin,
hurtling through space
in its race around the sun.
On the lunar surface,
mountains and valleys appear –
the heavenly bodies
no longer perfect and immutable.
Each planet assumes its rightful place
in its elliptical heliocentric orbit.
Jupiter acquires moons and Saturn rings.
The sun's face becomes spotted.
Stars retreat to unimaginable distances.
Wonders are revealed
more wonderful than those they displace
as old certainties crumble with
the authorities that supported them.
The universe starts divulging secrets
in the elegant poetry of mathematics.
People learn to measure, imagine,
experiment, observe,
and a later generation
sends people to the moon,
where a space-suited astronaut,
outside his lunar module,
drops a hammer and a feather together
and sees them hit the ground
simultaneously.

Labyrinth

I step into the design
formed on the ground
from sawn slices of trees
whose patterned rings reveal
the contours of life-spans
shaped by times and seasons
some showing signs
of damage and decay
a dignified guard of honour
as unhurriedly I tread
the sawdust-covered earth
held in the pattern's embrace
entrusting myself
to the mapped-out path
that gives shape and symmetry
to my life's journey
centring me
taking me to the heart

Lucky

for Graeme Marshall, dealer in Aboriginal art

I'm lucky to catch you.
On impulse, time rich, I drop in
to your gallery, hoping for a yarn.

At first, I seem to have missed you,
but I spend time with the paintings –
dramatic documents that
map myth, create country,
sung into being by artists
in desert communities
you've nurtured and learnt from.

Then, from the back of the shop,
I see you coming in
out of the summer heat –
but not sure, at first, if it's you,
the solid, dependable body
others have leaned on
now leaning on a stick,
unbalanced, unsteady.

Brain tumour, you tell me.
A year of intensive treatment,
two major operations.
And now yesterday's verdict,
from the latest scans,
that the rogue growth has spread.
Nothing more they can do.
A matter of months, maybe weeks.

And it's clear to me that
how you've lived your sixty years
has prepared you for this:
the honesty, the absence of pretence –
no counterfeit notes in your wallet –
a self-knowledge that has freed you
to be generously self-giving,
a life created on a large canvas,
with bold, assured brushstrokes,
the truthfulness and depth
of a Maringka Baker painting,
the colours humming with vitality,
the richly patterned story
whispering secrets of a far
but familiar country.

And I see that you are ready
for this final journey into the desert –
from which there will be no return –
where everything superfluous is dispensed with,
the outer layers shed,
leaving the essence to dissolve
into the light-drenched air
and the vast accepting earth.

And as I inwardly grieve
about how cruel life can be,
what a shocking hand you've been dealt,
I hear you speak, with your
usual conviction and passion,
no hint of anger, regret, self-pity,
of your outrageous good fortune in life,
how you see yourself as
the luckiest person alive.

Fence Music

on hearing about the Fence Project of Jon Rose,
composer, violinist, inventor of instruments

On a sand dune in the Strzelecki Desert
two musicians, shrouded in fly veils,
make music with violin bows
on the tensed wires of a fence

as they've done on fences across
the continent, recording sounds that vary
with the kind of wire (barbed or smooth)
its tension and length, its gauge and age

ethereal tones, luminously pure,
high in the cold sky of an outback night,
the scrape of wind on corrugated iron,
the noon throb of sun-steeped air

evocative of distance and drought,
isolation and loneliness,
a lament for lost species
and forests toppled for fence posts

the sonic story of taking possession
of an alien land, asserting ownership,
confining curved country
within straight lines

voicing *arco* the stand-off between
humankind and nature on the strings
of the world's biggest instrument –
five thousand kilometres of dingo fence

barbed music of the border barrier and
detention centre, elegiac protest against
fences everywhere that divide and exclude
discriminate and demean

I Can't Divine

I can't divine what hides behind your face,
can't get inside disguises you have made
or penetrate your hardened carapace.

I'd like to see you out in open space
not hunkered down behind your barricade –
I can't divine what hides behind your face.

I look to find some softening, just a trace,
but cannot cross the minefield you have laid
or penetrate your hardened carapace.

I'd gladly take you into my embrace
but when I try, my willing hands are stayed;
I can't divine what hides behind your face.

I cannot reach that core your fears encase,
I cannot get behind the roles you've played
or penetrate your hardened carapace.

I long to touch that tender wounded place
but cannot scale your well-built palisade.
I can't divine what hides behind your face
or penetrate your hardened carapace.

Fed

He sips his coffee in the shopping mall.
The eddying streams of shoppers flowing past
enclose him like a snug protective wall
behind which he can settle down at last
to tap the book of poems by his friend.
In the hubbub he finds calm, in the noise
an inner quiet. He roams the book from end
to end, delighting in its subtle joys.

He glances up. Nearby, serene, a mother
discreetly feeds her baby at her breast,
and in her private bliss he spies another
who's found this public space a place of rest.
He shuts the book and, rising from his seat,
steps back into the human flow, replete.

At the Dig Tree

They arrive,
these desert nomads,
riding modern-day dromedaries –
foreign-named, like Burke's camels:
Toyota, Nissan, Mitsubishi –
roof-rack packed with swags and extra tyre,
the back piled high with camping gear,
dusty, travel-hardened,
coming in off the inland sea of stones and sand
to this sacred site and its totemic cicatrised tree –
explorers in search of their own country,
looking for a story to claim as theirs,
seeking their own Dreaming.

The songlines of the Bandjigali and the Karenggapa –
the soft-footed ones who stepped lightly on the land
but deeply intuited its rhythms and wisdom –
are hard to discern now,
their outlines obliterated
by those who scarred the land with their hard soles
and heavy-footed animals.

The tree tells the travellers a story they recognise:
men battling heavy odds,
triumph turning to tragedy,
bad luck made worse by bad mistakes,
desolate deaths in a lonely landscape.

With their beasts of burden,
their wagon-loads of supplies,
their firearms and fish-hooks,
their writing on trees with steel not stone,
still some couldn't survive,
unable to recognise and benefit from
the land's generosity to others.

The visitors get back on board
and guide their ships of the desert
back to their Dreaming tracks –
Strzelecki, Birdsville, Cordillo –
resuming their quest
to penetrate the country's crust,
dig down far enough to find its heart,
but too recently arrived to do more
than scratch the surface.

A Plea

Dear God
complicate my world
make my thoughts subtle
give me nuanced perspectives
disturb my settled ways

deprive me of easy solutions
demolish my glib explanations
disrupt my black-and-white vision
keep me from being right

starve me of ready-made beliefs
upset my certainties
hide from me the truth
increase my doubt

banish me from the tribe
force me to fend for myself
send me on perilous journeys
put obstacles in my way

provide me with questions not answers
puzzle me with paradox
remain hidden from me
leave me wondering

To Soar

for Dorothy McKay

Here on the heights
at Stanwell Park, rugged up
against the eager breeze
that skips over the waves
far below, braces itself
for the sudden climb
then leaps up over the edge
of the cliff like a puppy
looking for someone to play with,

I recognise you in the woman
who starts down the slope
then is suddenly afloat
on the fathomless air,
playing chasey with the currents,
making sweeping turns
in search of updrafts' hidden pathways,
the kite's knife-edge slicing smoothly
through the sky's transparent waves.

It's here that I see you,
not in your hospice bed,
but spiralling in the lively air,
dancing with stately grace
in the arms of the spirited wind,
nursed by the earth's breath,
soaring the thermals
like a white-breasted sea-eagle
on upswept wings.

Not Unkind

It will be our last visit.
She looks so small in the hospital bed,
unnaturally still,
eyelids heavy,
lips trying to breathe a word or two,
the conquered body
using its last reserves
to close itself down.

Driving home,
the wipers sweeping
the rain-blurred windscreen,
we hear on the car radio
a discussion of A D Hope's poem
The Death of the Bird,
aired at this moment
seemingly just for us.

There's a sharp but healing
painfulness for us
in the bird's story.
Year after year
she has conquered the vast distance
from one hemisphere to the next
to make her nest
and tend her brood.

But now, small and frail
in the sky's expanse,
all her powers suddenly failing,
in mid-migration
she falters, then falls,
'and the great earth,
with neither grief nor malice,
receives the tiny burden of her death'.

And in the gift of this poem,
sent at the right time
to speak our thoughts for us
and ease us into our grieving,
we find that the world,
seemingly unfriendly
and indifferent to our fate,
is not unkind.

Rail Travellers

A melee of galahs,
fooling around as usual,
makes a rowdy show
of settling in a river red gum.
Learning language, I ask,
'What are they called?'
Graham hesitates.
'Er, might be *'ullococky?'*
We laugh. He suggests
I ask one of the old people.
I'm surprised he
can't give me a name.
The bird is common,
flaunting its presence,
not at all elusive like some.

It's old Jack who puts me
on the track of discovering
that this boisterous bird
with its Kamilaroi name
from the east coast
is a newcomer to the Centre,
a colonisers' collaborator,
extending its range
with the expansion
of grazing and agriculture
and the increased availability of water.
'That one,' says Jack. 'We don't
have a name for that one.
It came up with the railway line.'

And I savour the image
his words suggest
of a trainload of galahs,
behaving like idiots,
leaning backwards out of windows,
screeching with excitement,
setting out on a journey of
fifteen hundred kilometres
to their new home.

Deus Absconditus

Ascending skywards
seemed a good move.
From above the clouds
I reached down –
with unlimited power –
to whip up storms,
shake the earth,
take sides.

I was disturbed
by Copernicus et al,
who moved Earth
from the centre and then,
with their telescopes,
pushed me out
beyond the solar system,
among the stars.

Then Hubble, showing
Andromeda to be
a separate galaxy
outside the Milky Way,
thrust me into
intergalactic space
where I was
kept on the run

to the far reaches
of the universe,
back to the Big Bang,
where I tried to squeeze
into the first nanoseconds
but found there's
nowhere to hide
in a singularity.

I had no choice;
I returned to earth.
And I'm happy here,
back where I began,
in the place where
myth and metaphor meet,
having power
only to persuade,

lodged on the edge
of the liminal,
in the place of possibility,
at the point of connection,
hidden in
the flow,
the process,
the becoming.

Man on Wire

When I saw *Man on Wire*,
about the Frenchman
who secretly rigged a cable
between the Twin Towers in New York
and walked on it for 45 minutes,
450 metres above the ground,
what made me cry
was not only the audacity of it,
its implausibility,
but also its beauty.
For those who saw it,
it was an aesthetic experience,
a kind of poetry.
A policeman, sent to arrest him,
described it, not as tightrope walking,
but tightrope dancing.

I have done something audacious too.
Defying authority,
leaving the security of inherited faith,
I risked everything
and stepped out onto the wire.
Unsupported, free,
I experienced the elation
of finding equilibrium.
From the middle of the wire,
balancing,
I looked into the abyss
and did not fall.

Stealth

In a surprise attack
at ground level

the peregrine
makes its run

at high speed
across the wide

dry river bed
straight and unerring

like a missile
at no more than

knee height
coming in

under the radar
of the small birds

in the bush above
the washaway.

At the last
possible moment

it spears up over
the bank's lip.

The birds explode
from the bush.

The Wrong Grave

In the cemetery, standing around
in the warm winter sunshine
with seldom-seen relatives and friends,
having laid Wendy to rest
just short of her 61st birthday,
we feel thrust into a version of *Death at a Funeral*
when called together to be told
there's been a mistake
and she's been placed in the wrong grave.
The pallbearers,
doing overtime without complaint,
follow in the dignified footsteps of the undertaker
to transport her the hundred metres
to her proper resting place –
which we all agree is a much nicer spot,
and easier to find again later,
under the overarching branches of a slender gum tree.
Emptied of tears, we gather again,
a much smaller group than earlier,
concentrating on maintaining
a proper solemnity, as the pastor,
whose liturgy book prescribes
no ritual words for this eventuality,
improvises a prayer that makes
straight-faced mention
of life's ups and downs.

And it seems as if Wendy,
always thinking of others –
even on her deathbed apologising
in a barely audible whisper
for not being better company –
is nudging us back into the world,
relieving the gravity of our grieving,
comforting us with comic relief.

Birdwatching with St Francis

The ducks fly in low,
skidding on the water,
waddling up the stony shore.
For a moment I wonder
if they are congregating for a sermon,
but they forsake us for someone throwing breadcrumbs.

We head into the bush
and even the common species –
magpies, galahs, yellow-throated miners –
are an epiphany for him.
High in the branches of gum trees full of blossom
lorikeets converse in companionable creaks.

His first look through binoculars is such a shock
he would have dropped them
except for the strap around his neck.
It takes time for him to lose his fear of this devilish magic.
He finally gets the hang of focusing
and then won't let go of this magnifying miracle.

We shade our eyes from the weak winter sun
to follow a squadron of black cockatoos
slouching overhead in a plaintive fly-past.

I worry about his lack of shoes
as we follow the rocky track into the hills,
spying, as we go, on crested pigeons
a red wattlebird, a pair of red-rumped parrots,
but he shows no sign of discomfort.

Then, like an answer to prayer,
we find what I've been hoping for –
a family of blue wrens flitting and twitching
in the branches of a prickly acacia bush,
the colour-clad male coming close
in response to my lip-squeaking imitation
of a wren distress call.

On an open ridge
with a view over hills and valleys
to a patch of sea in the distance,
we sit on a log to eat our sandwiches,
blessed by the presence of a crimson rosella
in full view on the branch of a sapling.
We feast on its colour with our binoculars,
expecting a fleeting vision,
but it stays, and we resume our shared meal.

That time you preached to the birds …, I begin,
but he interrupts with an irritated shake of his head.
Pious legend, he says.
Followers always get things wrong.
The birds were preaching to me.
I was the one paying rapt attention.

Grass Hills

after the painting Grass hills, Tintaldra,
by Rupert Bunny 1926

This clean-cut landscape
rounded by erosion
baked like bread
in summer's oven
has contoured me
shaped my geography

We boys in summer
rode these slopes
on homemade sledges
their wooden runners
polished smooth as glass
by yellowed grass

And after years
of Europe's green
it's the gold and blue
of this lean landscape
lodged in my bones
that brings me home

Survival

Picking at the keyboard,
fossicking, I pause
to let my mind trawl
for an elusive phrase

and turn to find,
right under the window,
four crested pigeons
at work among the native plants

using their beaks
to disturb the top layer of mulch
with quick side-to-side
movements of their heads.

I'm impressed by their industry,
how they keep at it,
working this small patch
almost systematically

in spite of apparently
small pickings. Eventually
they leave and I resume
the painstaking

shaping of my poem,
working diligently
at what I need to do
to stay alive.

Gunyah Healing

gareth roi jones

gareth roi jones is the *nom de plume* of glen r johns.

Poetry is intensely personal, even when the events being described are put through the Alchemiac Truthifier all well-fired poetry should undergo. It is for this reason he prefers the refracted distance a pen name provides. (This is in fact the 4th name his poetry has been published under.)

That said, glen r has been a writer for 20 sommit years. Primarily as a playwright working with young people, but he's always dabbled in the poetical arts. He also has two unpublished children's novels he would like to remove the prefix from … & dozens more waiting to get out.

He currently runs a circus … which is as fun as it sounds (& fulfils a bunch of suggestions made to him as a kid!).

His dream job involves a combination of travelling, lying in hammocks reading books & drinking sauvignon blanc.

If anyone knows of such a job, please contact him ASAP.

Acknowledgements

Over my life I have had the privilege of loving & being loved by some amazing (amazing) women. I won't do them the dishonour of naming them here. Sadly I haven't always been mature or evolved enough to appreciate the wonders I'd been offered at the time they were given which caused myself, & no doubt them, varying degrees of pain for which I sincerely apologise. Luckily I always had *Gunyah* to go to heal. I hope they too had somewhere.

Thanks must go to Jenny & Ian, aka mum & dad (especially mum) for endless support, intermittent nagging & unstinting love. You really are lucky to live at *Gunyah* 24/7.

I've also been extremely blessed to have had all four of my grandparents (Ian & Valmai, Blue & Marj) for all my childhood & the majority of my adult life. You are in here.

Finally, thanks to Lara. You are at once: past, present & future. Thank you for returning to my heart & for the profoundly pleasant sensation you've given me – that of walking through life feeling like I'm constantly breaking into a smile …

PS Thanks for reminding me I am a poet. (If that's not worthy of a dedication, I dunno what is!)

Contents

The Keys to Everything

you lie still breath less
they give i take in a daze
think later don't want these
now all doors have closed
fat bunch of noisy bananas
metallic cumbersome overweight
nevertheless add to my own
severed lives symbolically rejoined
conglomerate sets of chaos
FrontdoorBackdoorScreendoor
YourCarMyCarTheShop
POBoxYourSistersPlace
ThePadlockOnTheShed
our individual additions of personality
– your plastic sunflower & red lips
– my bell which no longer tinkles
carry them with me always
though i have no desire
to unlock go get in anywhere anything ever again

Grandma Alcorn's Autopilot Stew

took time before
i could cook again
this first meal after

nothing major
wanting something simple
just a stew
instead of the carnage
which ensues

peeling potato i grate ice
dicing onion i dissect souls
cutting celery i crack vertebrae
everything has dark flavours
everything makes me weep
sadness my spice

Grandma Alcorn's vegetable stew
childhood favourite
now recipe of disaster

worse, in my delirium
i automatically prepare
enough for two

Plastic Shards

haven't heard music in months
so i spend all day listening
to favourite old cds

"i can't help falling in love"
"ain't love the sweetest thing"
"we get to carry each other"
"gonna love you till the seas run dry"
"i'll make you a star in my universe"

music by which we
met / married
danced / fought
made up / made love

"do you have to let me linger"
"must i dream & always see your face"
"these foolish games are tearing me apart"
"your shake is like a fish"
"if you wait, i will come for you"

break them all

"if i could through myself
set your spirit free
i'd lead your heart away"

plastic shards
shattering light into rainbows

Country Darkness

grew up sleeping in darkness
but a dozen years in the city
took away my edge
unused to night without light
night with no
– garish orange neon glow
– artificial illumination advertising pharmaceuticals & shoes
– headlights flicking across windows at 3 a.m.

unused to countrydark which envelops everything
covers all cracks, oozes into the crevices
hidden hollows & secret places of the soul
a dark so deep it drowns you in space
in a black hole within a blacker one
drifting without reference
even though the walls encase endless vacuums
so overwhelming it presses down on you
at the bottom of an eternal well
chestcrushing, forcing you to wheeze
at the impossibility of breath
only the rusty tinkle of an old windchime
reassures you are not lost in the void
& eventually sleep like a man drugged
plagued by livid heavy childlike dreams
all the while unable to suppress
the dull groggy fear you're at the end of all time

no wonder even the rooster
sounds relieved with the coming of the light

Milk Coffee

decadent creaminess
gives them divinity
addicted angels drink them
wings akimbo
after a tough day in heaven
this was long before i knew decadence
existed – let alone what it was

mum makes them before school
awesome on cold winter mornings
still sipping while being harangued
re tardiness all the way to the car
an expert in drinking *en route*
was once on the bus before realising
i hadn't left the mug on the back
seat of the Commodore as usual

because i snuggle in bed as long as possible
they always go cold & must be microwaved
before skimming the skin & sinking into sublimity
lost forever in the white goodness of milk
& the dark bliss of caffeine co-dependency

a frothy pseudo-cappuccino
a lifetime before becoming
an arts student & hearing the word *alfresco*

after abstaining for a score
i make myself one
20 years to figure out
they taste infinitely better fresh

New Paddock

the thrill of walking over land
which has been evolving & changing
for a million millennia
& for which we have
temporary custody
legally we have ownership
but that's too arrogant a phrase
for by rights we own it
as much as we own
the family of 3 kangaroos
which even now
is casually bounding away from us
heading west into the setting sun
clearing fencelines with nonchalant ease

our boundaries & definitions
arbitrary to them

Snake

a line of toxic oil
glistens multicolour black
black with rainbow prisms
quicksilverfast black
on the back verandah
spooking mum
sparking dad into action

that night they tell me
this is the first one
we've seen so close
to the house
since you were a kid

perhaps i draw
them to me
so i can listen
to their temptations

Clean Ghosts

coming home
exhausted
at day's end
startled by
a family line
of floating ghosts
freshly washed
hanging
under the verandah

after some seconds
my heartbeat
normalises
but the innocent
evening image
has done its damage
triggering
other spirits
less easily dismissed

Mauled Lamb

in the house paddock
not 50 yards from the backdoor
one of the new lambs freshly killed
guts gorged out
hollow beneath the ribcage
where once heart kidneys intestines
did their mysterious magic work
properly hidden from daylight eyes

when i came across it
the blood was still bright red
what's left of the lungs
rich as satin on a queen's throne
so fresh there weren't even flies
pockmarking the pink flesh
front legs perfectly positioned
as in a children's picturebook
white lamb gamboling over green grass
but the back legs
splayed 180° shockingly soft

a rogue dog? one of ours
or a whole pack?
Butch's too old, Alf too tiny
Jack's always tied up else he'll run away
Nugget's been aggressive
ever since the new pup arrived
bouncing & licking
his way into everyone's hearts

couldn't be Spike himself
at 14 months it's possible
but he's a baby, so surely not

all i know is dad says
something's going to pay
be it fox dog or human
a few months back
the neighbour's pitbull
went on a rampage
mauled 25 lambs & a ewe
paid $2250 compensation
that dog's been put down now

The First Frost

seven layers
still not enough

the (not-so) trusty potbelly
didn't last the night
the kitchen is ice

the coffee is innocuous
ineffective

step outside
& immediately
become a smoker

limbs refuse to function
have no fingers

white crackle is everywhere
every step is soundtracked
by breaking glass

eventually the sun
warms the air
enough to breathe

the chill forgotten
we remember how to talk

Splitting Wood

the secret every serious axewielder knows
(as instructed by father grandfather & papa alike)
to beat any piece of wood – first out-think it!
"brains not brawn"
"let the wood do the work"
"feel no pain, go with the grain"
etceteraing on into platitude infinity

woodsplitting as chess
it's man versus inanimate log
armed only with a stick & sharp steel wedge
strength enough to swing said wedge
& whatever native wit he possesses

the axe falls & returns like a rubber mallet
immediately bouncing back
my entire body reverberates
every vertebrae jarred silly

tenacious battle has been joined
between a stubborn General MacArthur
& a still-green-after-2-years redgum

sad how just a few minutes
violent futile slapstickfunny struggle
metamorphoses me from cocky 5-star general
to that hapless Athenian so out-of-breath after running
from Marathon to inform his *polis*
of their victory, he died on the spot

Small Cemetery

half a day's bike ride from *Gunyah*
a small disused cemetery
a relic from settler days
when the distance between
two points on a map was greater

a friend & i (was it Julian) picnicked there
once long ago enticed by an Enid Blyton style
Famous Five inspired English adventure
ripping good fun, eh what, squire?
what we didn't count on
was a blistering Australian summer day
heatexhausted by the time we arrived

in our canvas backpacks
the curried egg sandwiches had gone off
the gingerbeer was almost boiling
& the tinned lamb tongue melted into goop

instead we siestaed the heat away telling
feeble ghost stories under old cypress trees
surrounding WILLHEIM WÖBBELDOLCH's grave
till evening breezes cooled us
enough to brave the journey home

when i told the story you laughed
said we should recreate the odyssey
one clear lasercrisp blue autumn afternoon

today i notice my first leaf falling

Re: Birth

my sister's water broke
as she was setting a client's perm
understandably a flurry of panic followed

after 9 months & 2 days
of impenetrable patience
(barely a kick, so we were told)
placid & placable
suddenly my niece is ready
uncurling from inside my sibling's belly
a small pink shoot stretching from bloodred soil

joy is everywhere
my parents (tears in eyes, laughing)
are grandparents at last
theirs, great-grandparents all
gran clapping her hands
the joyous way she does

i alone am deserted
bitterly reminded of two sets of keys

the elder who should've been a father
years ago & now never will

Prolapsed Ewe

the neighbour's kids
build an elaborate system
of dams canals & waterfalls
(worthy of any foreign ricepaddy)

while my father & their mother
cram a young ewe's
reproductive organs
back inside where they belong
(she prolapsed while lambing)

i bystand
(feeling as awkward & useless
as a man in a chickensuit
giving out flyers to CAGED EGGS R US
to unreceptive shoppers
at an organic farmers market)

the kids show occasional interest
in the gory goings on
but are generally more amused
by their ever-increasing mudbath
(the obsessive love-affair between children & dirt)

on the other hand i am gawkeyed
fascinated by the red rock
melon sized satellite
pockmarked lunar surface
that is her insideout uterus

intrigued by the way
ordinary white refined sugar
shrivels the moon
to a third its original size
& slightly sickened
as they sew her up
using safety pins & dental floss

five pairs of hands
two covered in mud
two in blood
one clean

Hot Gully Winds

down from the hills in October
the cool tan hills
come the gully winds

hot   dry   short   sharp   fast

you believe
you own these winds
that they are yours, you theirs
when they come in October
(when they come in other months
no doubt they belong to others)

but when they come in October
they are yours
tugging your red mane, slapping your face
& cleaving your arms out from your sides
making you believe you can fly

when they came in October
when they came hot
hot blasts of bushfired air
when they came at the end
of long pre-summer days
after the land has sweltered & scorched
under their touch

i believed they came to melt you
too late i learnt
it was i who needed melting

Drenching: The Lesson

working the mob in the yards
moving them into the race
Nugget is a reluctant crowdsurfer
balancing on woolly backs
like a circus act

sometimes he seems to love it
lightly skipping like black lightning
othertimes scared of slipping
as the sea beneath his paws parts

the ewes certainly don't appreciate
a dog riding sidesaddle on their spines
& run along the race as requested
when full, dad starts drenching

these are old girls
due for the ship this year
after 6 or 7 years repeatedly
popping out little lambikins
which we either keep as ewes
or neuter & fatten for market
a cruel reward
for a lifetime of service
a farm is a brutal place
but it reinforces
life either goes on

or it doesn't

Fire

not a bonfire with close friends
drinking beer laughing at dumb jokes
roasting marshmellows telling ghost tales
but a hard work fire
hot sweaty work

a grandpa pine gave up its footing
during a recent southerly

when dad set it this afternoon
the stubborn old stump didn't burn
to encourage its combustion
i relocated coals with a shovel
crowbarred halfburnt logs closer
raked in loose twigs & cones

once done i sit back
in the glow & rest
watching flame
fascinated
as we always are

contemplating
primal origins of the species
savouring our obsession
since caveman days
with being burnt away

mesmerised by the evershifting
swirlstorm of firecracker sparks
which (after my labours)
crackle most satisfyingly
popcorn exploding in a pan
100 angry whips cracking staccato
shotgun cracks echoing in the gums

playing pick-a-spark
following one into the stars
tracing its chiffon tail
hoping the chosen one goes highest
dreaming of flight

remembering how when younger
(a long time ago)
i used to sit in darkness
& do exactly this
this is not *déjà-vu*
it is the same moment

from far away i hear my mother laugh

Early Morning

light unravels
(the mystical unpeeling
of an enormous orange)
shakes off frost
burns mist
& squeezes shadows
out of valleys

so this is dawn

Morning Cuppa

the full deep flavour of English Breakfast tea, ironically
reminds me of Australian country kitchens, circa 1950

big wooden table veneered by starchwhite cloth
weighted with food into forevers past
fried rinds of thick bacon (no vacwrap in sight)
a rockpile of softcentred eggs (genuine freerange)
& toast soldier accompaniment (solid chunky waifless)
freshly squeezed juice (still with seeds pulp taste)
freshly squeezed milk (still warm, homogeniswhat?)
rich yellow butter (no added canola for easy spreading)
raggededged homemade bread (no waferthin preslicing)

everything cradled cupped or encased
by heavyduty blue&white crockery
half an inch thick & dispatched with bonehandled
cutlery the size of swords pitchforks spades

the jar of VEGEMITE & the KELLOGS cornflakes
the only concessions to the existence
of an outside world

which explains why
(even though i never lived then
– this is my parents' breakfast
– its virtues relived in endless litany)
my morning cuppa
of royal red English Breakfast
is a meal in itself

For a Moment, a Child Again

sitting on a verandah
in daylight saved sun
spitting watermelon seeds
into a long shaggy lawn
just for fun

Exaltation of the Mandarin

reluctant to leave the tree
so flick the wrist

pierce the goosebumpled skin
with a grimy nail

a minicloud of citrus mist
bursts forth

sniff it taste it
the tang of freshness

crescent moons containing
sweet beads of flesh

beneath their thin
rubbery skin

eat the ambrosia
savour it

in a twinkling of exuberance
i hurl the remnants in the air

a sunshower of rind
scatters over the garden

So Close to the Milky Way

with constellations close enough to touch
it's no wonder as a child i believed i could
command stars to fall just by wishing
i'd step off the verandah into the vineyard
& before taking a hundred steps
the air above me would *whoosh!*
i'd even command what quadrant they fell
& be disappointed if wrong

once i had a girlfriend who lived in the city
& when she visited she said
she'd never seen a shooting star
i laughed at that
it was the last summer we were together

another year a meteor shower
made me wake my parents at 3 a.m.
to see huge streaks of magnesium whites
copper blues titanium silvers & sodium yellows
turn our backsky into a sublime personal pyrotechnica
that still thrills me to this day thinking about it

but i'm an adult now my power long gone
now they're just stars, common garden –

whooooooooosh!
(right through Pleiades: the Bull's Tail)
– about time i've been waiting almost an hour

relieved i head back inside

In Praise of Gum Trees

when young we think ourselves wise
when we know nothing
arrogance unimaginable superiority complexes galore
yet lessons will be learnt
a personal arrogance was anti-Australianism
belief that anywhere everywhere else was better
this even extended to the most innocent of locales
the creeks & plains, hillsides & glens which accommodated
Genus Eucalyptus: the humble gum

i found beauty in beeches, oaks, elms, poplars, willows
deciduous Europeans held sway, glamoured me
with vibrant baby greens, lush verdant leaves
glorious autumnal golds, reds & yellows
& stark emperorial majesty when naked
gums were ugly graceless grotesque gargoyles
misshapen mishmashes of twigs, bark, gnarls & knobs
dull limp olivecolour leaves hanging too lazy to move
relentlessly dropping sticks even whole limbs on hot days

but time spent in the city & overseas humbled me
now i cannot gaze upon gums without wistful nostalgia
without longing indeed
without love for their speckled shade
mix of rough bark over smooth skin multicolour leaves
musical windrustle & dogged perseverance
in the face of El Niño, mistletoe & bad farming practice

at night lying next to the window
in this my childhood room
i am well covered in eucalypt dreams

The Vegie Patch

too common a phrase to describe
the microcosmos before me
in my washed out amber Polaroid youth
it was a simpler affair
chicken mesh & a few rough gum posts
a rectangle of rustic practicality
bordered by pampas grass & a dour lemon tree
not the architectural worldwonder it is today
raised beds bordered by moss rocks
handpicked from the paddocks
several shiny new galvanised half rainwater tanks
espalier fruit trees: plum, a Josephine pear
apricot, lemon & Bonzer apple (great name, lousy eating)
this year alone growing
corn, cauliflower, cucumber, broccoli, onion, tomato

as a child i hated tomato
couldn't force me to eat it if you tried
but as an adult adore it
unsure when that seismic shift occurred
but i recall standing in latesummer sunshine
crepuscular light shafts
columning the clouds like a Hellenic temple
(you are in the hammock reading *Middlemarch* again
arms wilting under the weight)
& biting
into a stillwarm sweetsmelling freshlypicked Grosse Lizzie
ambrosia, nectar, manna etc (all the words appear)
red juice drippling down my chin
& thanking god that life couldn't get any better than this

The Flower of the Sun

the smell of summer
on your wrists the day we met
   scent still in my heart

Sliding Down the Belly of the World

Rachael Mead

Rachael lives on a property in the Adelaide Hills with her husband, animals and an unwieldy collection of op shop overcoats. She's currently juggling managing a second-hand bookshop with completing her Ph.D. in creative writing at the University of Adelaide. She has an Honours degree in Classical Archaeology, a Masters in Environmental Studies and has worked for the last decade as an environmental and animal rights campaigner for organizations such as Greenpeace, the Greens, the Conservation Council of SA and Animal Liberation SA.

Her poetry has been published in journals such as *Meanjin*, *Westerly*, *Going Down Swinging* and the *Australian Poetry Members Anthology*. In 2011 she was a Friendly Street mentored poet with Mike Ladd and she spent three weeks in residence at Varuna, The Writers' House in the Blue Mountains as the recipient of the Dorothy Hewett Flagship Fellowship for Poetry.

Acknowledgments

Poems in this collection have appeared in *SWAMP*, *Poetrix*, *Animate Quarterly III* and *Animate Quarterly IV* and *InDaily* Poets' Corner.

My sincere thanks to Kate Deller-Evans for selecting this manuscript. / Deep gratitude to Jude Aquilina, Jill Jones and Mike Ladd for their generous mentorships, Thom Sullivan for editorial savvy and Maggie Emmett for boundless faith and encouragement. / Thank you Friendly Street Poets – what a priceless South Australian institution. / For friendship, support and clear-eyed editing, special thanks to the gorgeous ladies of the yet-to-be-officially-named poetry group – Cass Flanagan Willanski, Jules Winefield and Heather Taylor Johnson. For love and unwavering belief – thank you Jess Gilding. / Thanks and appreciation to Aspen Medical in the Solomon Islands, Trixie Woodill and Michael Peek in Christchurch, Gateway Antarctica at the University of Canterbury, Antarctica New Zealand and the folk at Scott Base. / To Jim Giles (1931–2010), who was the first person to like my poems while being under absolutely no obligation to do so, thank you for your hearty, steadfast support. You are sorely missed. / Heartfelt thanks to my unofficial patrons, Vee and Denis Noble. You are unfailingly supportive, always toast my successes with multiple bottles of champagne and let me ferret around in your stationery cupboard without raising an eyebrow. / Thanks to Mum and Dad for instilling in me a love of words and never complaining about my nose being continually lodged in a book (except at the dinner table which I still consider to be the height of injustice.) / And finally, to the one to whom I owe everything – Andrew Noble. My love. Thank you doesn't even come close.

Contents

Honiara Morning

The grass broom scritches by
All is weighted with green
The sea takes deep breaths
Palms air their parasols

All is weighted with green
Spray varnishes the air
Palms air their parasols
Sweat films the skin

Spray varnishes the air
Mangoes tense like dew
Sweat films the skin
Frangipani sieves the breeze

Mangoes tense like dew
The sea takes deep breaths
Frangipani sieves the breeze
The grass broom scritches by

Heliophile

Nine degrees south of the Equator,
I'm perched on
the full belly of the world.
At noon I go outside to find my love,
feel her sharp gaze on my skin.
I'm so close to her here,
closer than I've ever been.
She's transformed me,
branded now with a pale bikini.
I crave her touch all over
but to keep up appearances
I'm staying conservatively clad.

I just can't keep away from her,
watching her gaudy dives and surfacings from the sea.
All day I'm entranced by her white hot proximity.
Her closeness quickens my breath,
I flush and sweat.
Obsessively, I circle her.
The whole world is in her thrall.
She just smiles and teases,
dancing towards me, then away.
Every day the same act
but I can't resist.
Without her I'm nothing
and she knows it.

Guadalcanal

It's not like those war documentaries
viewed through the glassed distance of space and time
with the colours of ocean and jungle saturated and framed
    like polaroids
only the surface captured, only the bravado
while the fear and tension remained inexpressible, unrecorded
but what's left behind speaks of those boys being just like us
with reading glasses, coke bottles, forks, teeth with fillings
bringing them back to us not just as soldiers
but with their unbreakable humanity bursting through
we can hear them singing to the radio, talking of home,
    laughing with friends
sensed now only in the tinny distance
the truth of it taken into death
the truth of it to be endured on long nights kept company
    only by whiskey
brave and scared, they were just like our brothers
loud and shy, quick and slow, greedy and giving
good and evil
a universal equation that will never be balanced
all skin sacks of nature destined to decompose
some lie in the grassed graves of home
some lie here on the littered jungle carpet
she is a surrogate mother with her own traditions
taking as sons those lost boys
she holds them close to her shadowed breast.

She holds them close to her shadowed breast
taking as sons those lost boys
she is a surrogate mother with her own traditions
some lie here on the littered jungle carpet
some lie in the grassed graves of home
all skin sacks of nature destined to decompose
a universal equation that will never be balanced
good and evil
loud and shy, quick and slow, greedy and giving
brave and scared, they were just like our brothers
the truth of it to be endured on long nights kept company
    only by whiskey
the truth of it taken into death
sensed now only in the tinny distance
we can hear them singing to the radio, talking of home,
    laughing with friends
but with their unbreakable humanity bursting through
bringing them back to us not just as soldiers
with reading glasses, coke bottles, forks, teeth with fillings
but what's left behind speaks of those boys being just like us
while the fear and tension remained inexpressible, unrecorded
only the surface captured, only the bravado
with the colours of ocean and jungle saturated and framed
    like polaroids
viewed through the glassed distance of space and time
it's not like those war documentaries.

The Wreck

The wind flings waves upon the calm.
In the shallows the fins and mask are awkward.
How ridiculous in this element we are,
voyeurs peering through the rippled lens of ceiling.
The darting natives mock us with their diminutive grace.
They flick past, colourful as Californians, indifferent as
    New Yorkers.

Light beams through, azure fabric shot with gold.
Curtains of fish sway in unpredictable breezes
then flick aside to reveal the wreck,
a new city rising from the ruins of the past.
The hull tilts into coral, life pours with it
rolling away into cobalt
leaving this cathedral, a precarious nave
with arms arching for the mercurial horizon.
The velvet waft and drag of anemones, the leadlight coral,
a fractal patchwork of worlds within worlds.
The wreck content with this new incarnation,
procreation vanquishing destruction.

The solemn cadence of snorkel breath, the powerful finning,
this mythic perspective of undersea flight
transforms us into priestesses of this grotto.

With hair a storm of seaweed, muscular flukes fanning,
we are hybrids of Eve and the Virgin,
pleasure coiled within virginal trepidation of the unknown,
    unseen.
We are without tongue, but with movement sing pure
    enchantments,
echoing back to the dawn of time when we came from
    the sea.

Emerging from the ocean,
we are visions of wave and spray,
still speechless.

Liminal Refuge

House floods off the verandah
and cascades down the steps
while garden clambers up and over the porch
ivy romances the posts
plants mingle in corners.

A shadowed place during brightness
but a sanctuary of light in the dark
it brings the outdoors inside
yet encloses us while out.

In the candlelit dusk
with the stereo playing poetry
plants and chairs
regard each other
with English reserve
this verandah
a peaceful balance of worlds
a haven for indecision.

Choosing Wallpaper with Virginia Woolf

It's not easy.
Virginia's very fond of what I call institutional green
and although I submitted to her about the living room
she'd prefer it throughout
and just won't listen when I say it would be like living
    underwater.
And please don't get her started on wallpaper.
She may look a bit Pre-Raphaelite
but don't be fooled and start talking up William Morris.
She can practically snort the word "Newnham" out her nose
and mentioning a predilection for rustic or artisan creations
is a mistake if you don't want to be ridiculed
behind your back to Bloomsbury.

Emily Dickinson and I don't see eye to eye
on interior design either.
Why does everything have to be white?
With that taste for simplicity and function
she really should've been a Shaker.

And Simone de Beauvoir is no help at all.
If it was up to her
all I'd own is a desk and a chair
and even then she'd recommend
doing all my writing in a café anyway.

Now Diego Rivera appreciates me
and not just because I look like his wife.
If he had his way
I'd probably have a few more politically inspired murals
but he gives my colours and cacti the nod
and really loves my affinity for arum lilies.

But actually
I think my decorating soul mate must be Alice Walker
and although I haven't painted a room purple
or the exterior of my house azure blue yet
we agree on the fundamentals.
Each room vibrating with colour,
every object offering a story
and the garden
a room of one's own.

Change

You can't tell people to turn off lights.
And saying they should walk more
and buy less at the mall doesn't work either.

You've just got to trust that one day
they will be caught breathless
by a moment
when the sun refracts just so
through a hanging raindrop
or by a clatter of parrots taking flight.

When a sleepless night becomes a vigil
with the dawn song of a magpie.
When watching a sunset
or the gentle touch of bee to bloom
makes time slow like honey.

You have to trust that
this will become the sacred moment.
That this second of recognition
of their place in the great family
will become the foundation
upon which every subsequent decision
must rest
then sit comfortably.

Isn't that how it happened for you?

Still Life

Each day I practice the art
of arranging a still life
then residing within,
composing the room,
how the light caresses it,
how this space will be seen.

Spurred by the industrial truth
of life's steady factory
whose only product is the grave.
Time mocks Zeno's paradox
of infinite divisions
between zero and one.
Zero is always possible, inevitable.
Those endlessly small divisions
between death and life
are days.

I arrange myself in today's still life,
cradled by chair, dogs pooled below.
The house my shell,
my country and universe.
The doorway tenderly holds its garden.

These poems trying to catch time
and hold it still;
the light, the wind, the seasons,
this moment a still life
unframed,
flapping in memory's draughts.

Bask

I lie when people ask me
why I am so brown.
I spend a lot of time in the garden, I say,
I ride my bike to work.
And I guess these are not completely untrue
but they are not the whole reason why I am so brown
or why the tan flows seamlessly under my clothes.
These days I am scared to admit
that I often lie naked under the sun
kept company by Mary Oliver or Sylvia Plath,
so pale I need sunglasses to look at them.
I know full well that this is truly stupid
for an Australian woman
who doesn't want to die of melanoma
before her skin even has a chance to crinkle
like desert sands.
But somewhere within lurks reptilian DNA,
the overwhelming desire to bask,
an ancient knowing of the sun as energy,
recharging me for the unrelenting hours
spent in dim interiors
lit only by the blue-white glare,
with my sole companion
the despair of a world gone awry.

Reflections

You came to dinner last night
and had flattened me
before you even arrived.

As we ate
you talked
your words inflating you, rounding you out, creaseless
while I diminished to a sliver of foil
reflecting you
shining your image back
for you to admire.

And finally I see it.
I'm your mirror
reflecting
the vision of yourself you want to see,
larger and more beautiful than you really are.

No wonder you didn't want to know me
when I cracked.
It distorted the image
like carnival glass,
warping the light that shone from you.
Suddenly I was a tarnished spot
to be polished off.

I'm so thankful we didn't end up travelling together.
I would've been so thin from the constant polishing,
beaming you larger than life
into strangers' eyes
I would've disappeared completely.
A mirror is after all mostly glass.
Or more cracks would've appeared

and by god
I probably would've ended up killing you
off a whisper of a dirt track in the desert,
hunkered down under the open night
cracking your bones for the marrow
the ochre fire
reflecting
your grease
on my chin.

The Metal Detector

A heatwave morning, 6 a.m.
My husband jettisoned at the airport
for an anthropological field trip
to see AC/DC in Melbourne.

At Henley Square
it's still dark
and the streetlights curve,
pastel sequins beading
the hem of coast to Seacliff.

Sovereignty of this dark beach
has been claimed by the fit.
They emerge from the obscure
with and without dogs,
passing with swift cadence
through the cool lamplight of the Square.

Dual rows of boot campers,
skin already shining,
crunch and lunge on the grass.
Military exhortations wheel in the wind like gulls.
I'm the only one here sneakerless
with untamed hair.

The sea is far too energetic for dawn.
It has no colour, just opacity
and the raw blisters where my feet spurn shoes
burn in the salt.

The idea of day makes the hills blush
but I have no tolerance for such modesty
at this hour.
All this puritanical health
is an alienation,
a distance not measured by map.

Finally someone else unconcerned with longevity appears.
He sweeps the beach systematically
head dipped in concentration
under the pincer grip of earphones.

He inhabits another world
attuned to other rhythms
than the crash and bleed of the sea.
Sweep, step
Sweep, step.
The sun stretches awake
under the blanketing hills
while both of us
detector and pen in hand
methodically
mine the beach
for gold.

My Kind

We are foreigners in our own lands
Feel home as more than a house
Our family extends beyond the human

My kind see forests as temples
Know money to be a tin god
Hear media as just another voice

We are not people of crossed fingers
Knowing hope is not a strategy
And that civilisation rocks on unsteady feet

We are insomniacs, shards of the night
Unkempt and filthy, decadent and superb
Our watches tell geological time

Compassionate and bountiful, mad and brilliant
We speak the languages of the voiceless
And know the Earth by her true name

We are dangerous and powerful
Present in light and shadows
Not uniformed, we hide in plain sight

You know us

Travelling to Antarctica

i. hailstone moon

Tonight the hailstone moon
is full over Christchurch.
By the time she melts
I will be in a land without night
almost standing on the moon
with no sight of her
to prove me wrong.

ii. ice and radishes

The last night in Christchurch
toes in the grass
eating crimson radishes
tender from the soil.
Suspended now on solid cold
earth invisible below
it is an effort to recall
that this iced cup
holding the globe
drives the oceans and atmosphere
allowing plump radish toes
to snuggle deep in quilted soil
back in Christchurch.

The Day Is Done

The ice kitchen is functional
(except for a small but unerring draught)
dinner has been made, eaten
and the dishes wiped clean
the greywater has been downed
with a toast and a grimace
the ice for drinking tomorrow
has been melted and stored
the kitchen and stove boxes
are packed and tied down
close and secure
in case of blizzard
the polar tent is tidy
the food bag sorted
and lunch for tomorrow's field work
identified and packed

finally a breath on my own time

the windproof salopettes go on
over the merino longjohns
then the thermal shirt and vest
now the extreme weather jacket
and neck gaiter
but where is my notebook?
in my pocket, check
then a coat of sunscreen
before polartech gloves
and ear-protecting headband
under a thick beanie
then a minute for the mukluks
and straightening up outside the tent
is the place for sunglasses
and windproof gloves
only to find in the time it has taken
to dress for the occasion
the wind has come in from the Pole
there will be no wandering into silence

brain and body cool with disappointment
while undressing down to new synthetic skin
eyes close to create artificial night
in the sleepless day.

The Shovel Up

a day of bright nautical stripe
gloveless and sweating
building snow castles
on the ocean of ice

women shovel a blizzard
into a building
laughter binding the dome
harmony carving the lintel

under Erebus' clear eye
we lean on tools aglow
the whiteout for which we prepare
far over our minds' horizon

Sestina Antarctica

Beauty seizes the soul and squeezes it deep
Passing of time is a trick of the light
Horizon marks the edge of an ocean of ice
With dragon backs surfacing from a mantle of white
Katabatics fall off the base of the world
Mountains of cloud cloak the rim of the Sound

Stark mountain skeleton embossed on the Sound
Black nunatak punctures the powdered sky deep
Binary contrast defining this world
Porcelain wind showers splinters of light
Not absence of colour but spectrum of white
From silver through purple, a palette of ice

Glacier's edge, ruined city of ice
Directing the wind and conducting the sound
Range bound together with smoothest of white
Resolute in time, standing lofty and deep
Through seasons of dark, seasons of light
Honouring memory from dawn of the world

Texture becomes colour in a minimal world
Eyes learning to read from a text of ice
Snowflakes fill footprints, turn heavy steps light
Taste of relief in each step safe and sound
Snapping red flags dwindle into the deep
Polar tent monuments in desert of white

Icicles trap blue in a prison of white
Discordant wind engulfs pale lunar world
In abyss of sound human voices chime deep
Crampons leave tracks of clawed beasts on the ice
Ripping the silence with high tensile sound
Skuas smear shadows on infinite light

Erebus, a deity rising from light
Angle of sun reveals texture of white
Mountains like fingers grip edge of the Sound
Arresting a slip from the rim of the world
Scrabbling nails claw at the smooth lip of ice
Soon to lose purchase, plunging into the deep

Midnight light glows on the nacreous world
A sestina of white in a language of ice
The Sound freezes silent, mountains solemn and deep.

Sound

McMurdo Sound is silent
snowflakes chatter
down the fluttering road
flags snap percussion to the melody of wind

snowflakes chatter
while crampons scritch on ice
flags snap percussion to the melody of wind
triple beat of crampons then ice axe

while crampons scritch on ice
rare moment leached by exclamation
triple beat of crampons then ice axe
snow ticks by like sand

rare moment leached by exclamation
down the fluttering road
snow ticks by like sand

McMurdo Sound is silent

Coping with Christchurch

Traffic an ocean rhythm
for pelagic urban species
in flashing shoals
of beige tourists
netted with cameras.
The neon repulsing,
no haven on the mercantile reef
for this hermit crab.
Her pearl shell interior
both respite and reminder
of the lost cold world.
The sun once constant companion
now fleeting friend.
She grieves for the frozen ocean
of her personal continent.

The World at My Feet

Finally, their patience has been repaid
and after years of embarrassed disdain
I have fallen in love with my feet.
In an inconsistent culture
that prizes slender tapers for fingers
but stout regimented toes,
I've been blinded to their primate beauty.
Footprints like continents
with a Somalian bunion,
Cape Corn,
a deep Amazonian basin
and a Guyana so long it's a peninsula.
Soil brown and bordered with sand,
clouds, birds and leaves have lost their charm.
I only have eyes for the New Worlds below.

Friendly Street New Poets Series

Friendly Street New Poets 10 (2004)
Stealing · Libby Angel
Deaf Elegies (from Virginia Woolf's Record Store) · Robert J. Bloomfield
Sparrow in an Airport · rob walker

Friendly Street New Poets 11 (2005)
low background noise · Cameron Fuller
words free · Simone G. Matthews
jars of artefacts · Rachel Manning

Friendly Street New Poets 12 (2006)
The Night is a Dying Dog · Steve Brock
Travelling · Margaret Fensom
Nectar and Light · Murray Alfredson

Friendly Street New Poets 13 (2007)
Black Magic · Courtney Black
Circus Earth · Janine Baker
Hieroglyphs · Roger Higgins

Friendly Street New Poets 14 (2008)
Snatching Time · M.L. Emmett
The Boy Full of Broken Promise · Rob Hardy
Airborne · Thom Sullivan

Friendly Street New Poets 15 (2009)
A Lesson in Being Mortal · Louise McKenna
A Pause in the Conversation · Lynette Arden
Natural Intervention · Sher'ee Furtak-Ellis

Friendly Street New Poets 16 (2010)
Voyages to Another Planet · John Brydon
Mistaken for a Real Poet · Mike Hopkins
Glowing in the Dark · Simon J. Hanson

website: friendlystreetpoets.org.au
email: poetry@friendlystreetpoets.org.au
postal: PO Box 3697 Norwood SA 5067